The Great Flood

How Sheffield, Rotherham, Barnsley, Doncaster, Chesterfield and Worksop survived the summer storms of 2007

**Compiled and written by
Martin Smith**

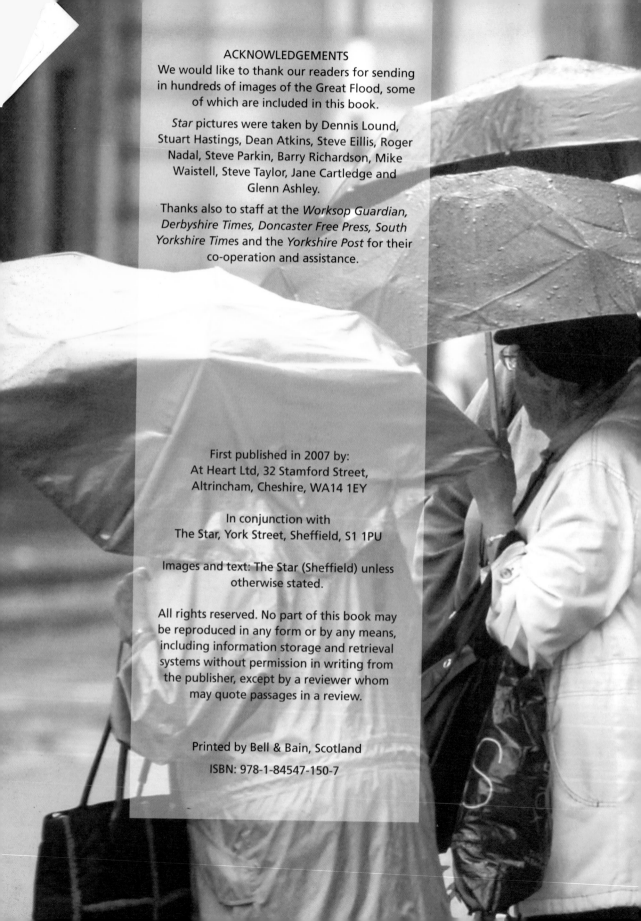

ACKNOWLEDGEMENTS
We would like to thank our readers for sending in hundreds of images of the Great Flood, some of which are included in this book.

Star pictures were taken by Dennis Lound, Stuart Hastings, Dean Atkins, Steve Eillis, Roger Nadal, Steve Parkin, Barry Richardson, Mike Waistell, Steve Taylor, Jane Cartledge and Glenn Ashley.

Thanks also to staff at the *Worksop Guardian, Derbyshire Times, Doncaster Free Press, South Yorkshire Times* and the *Yorkshire Post* for their co-operation and assistance.

First published in 2007 by:
At Heart Ltd, 32 Stamford Street,
Altrincham, Cheshire, WA14 1EY

In conjunction with
The Star, York Street, Sheffield, S1 1PU

Images and text: The Star (Sheffield) unless otherwise stated.

Printed by Bell & Bain, Scotland
ISBN: 978-1-84547-150-7

CONTENTS

DEDICATION

This book is dedicated to the memory of

Ryan Parry
and
Peter Harding
of Sheffield

and
Gary Priestley
of Clowne

who died in the Great Flood of 2007.

INTRODUCTION

THE great flood of 2007 will go down in the history of South Yorkshire, north Nottinghamshire and North East Derbyshire as one of our worst ever natural disasters.

Three died, thousands were evacuated to safety and thousands more made homeless by floods caused by the wettest June since records began.

Monday June 25 was simply astonishing. Rivers broke their banks, roads, homes, shops and businesses were flooded, cars, trees, walls and fences swept away by a torrent our waterways just could not cope with.

The rain in the days preceding the bursting of the rivers Don, Sheaf, Rother, Ryton and Hipper was exacerbated by the torrential downpour of the previous two weeks, flooding parts of Barnsley, Rotherham and Sheffield.

The streams and rivers and the region's underlying water table were already full. There was nowhere for the extra water to go.

And what a downpour.

Hour after hour, day after day of tropically intense rain fell on the region. There could only be one result.

In the days that followed there were many tales of heroism, tragedy and defiance in the face of almost insurmountable problems.

For six days and beyond *The Star* was filled with images and written accounts of disaster, tragedy and triumph and above all of the indomitable spirit and courage of the people of this region.

Through the words and pictures in this book we hope to illustrate and describe some of those stories and that singular determination to beat the odds.

The cost of recovery and reconstruction will run into many millions and the area will need special assistance from national Government to battle back.

But as surely as we survived the floods, we will rebuild and regenerate our region.

THE DELUGE

DAY 1: After the wettest weekend in the wettest June on record we were hit by more rain of devastating intensity.

On Monday June 25, 2007, it fell with apocalyptic menace all day and into the night.

No-one had ever seen anything like it. There was a widespread realisation something extraordinary was happening.

Late that afternoon the River Don burst its banks in the centre of Sheffield and the road through the Lower Don Valley from the Wicker to Meadowhall became a roaring torrent of water.

The Sheaf burst its banks in Millhouses Park and claimed the life of 14-year-old Ryan Parry who was playing in the floodwaters with his friends on the way home from school.

Peter Harding, aged 68 from Burngreave was swept away when he got out of his car in Newhall, Sheffield. Ex-policeman Gary Priestley, from Clowne, died as he tried to get home.

In 12 hours South Yorkshire Fire and Rescue received 1,500 calls – the daily average is just 159.

Around 200 residents were evacuated from Winn Gardens in Sheffield and the Lower Don Valley. Meadowhall Interchange was closed, there was an explosion at Firth Rixson. Rotherham, Barnsley and areas of Doncaster were hit by their second floods in ten days.

By 10pm firefighters throughout the county had 73 live incidents and a further 126 incidents in the queue to be attended.

A fire at Neepsend electricity substation left 35,000 residents and numerous businesses without power.

The region became the centre of worldwide media attention as a massive rescue operation was launched in the Sheffield district of Brightside where more than 100 workers were plucked from the roofs of flooded buildings by three RAF helicopters.

"It truly is a disaster for Sheffield," said Attercliffe MP Clive Betts.

Sir Bob Kerslake, chief executive of Sheffield City Council, said: "We have seen the most intense rain since records began.

"This has been quite unparalleled and extraordinary. People who have lived all their lives in Sheffield would say this is the most severe flooding they've ever seen."

Areas of Chapeltown, Ecclesfield, Worksop and Chesterfield were also under water with devastating consequences. Ulley Reservoir was becoming perilously swollen.

Two dead, hundreds trapped as city counts the cost of worst downpour in living memory

Flood victim Ryan Parry, aged 13

Picture: Steve Ellis

Flood of tears

Flooding in Sheffield – Thorncliffe Industrial Estate, Chapeltown, one driver had to abandon his vehicle after trying to make it through flooding. The flood waters later rose and almost totally submerged the vehicle. (Picture taken by Paul David Drabble)

Battling through. Flooding in Church Street, Ecclesfield, Sheffield. (Picture taken by Paul David Drabble)

Submerged ground floor
apartments at Hillsborough.

Firefighters rescue OAP's
Don and Rose Ford from
their Ecclesfield home.

After the River Don burst its banks on Saville Street, Sheffield.

Taken from The Wicker Arches Bridge looking towards the Don Valley.

Floods on The Wicker.

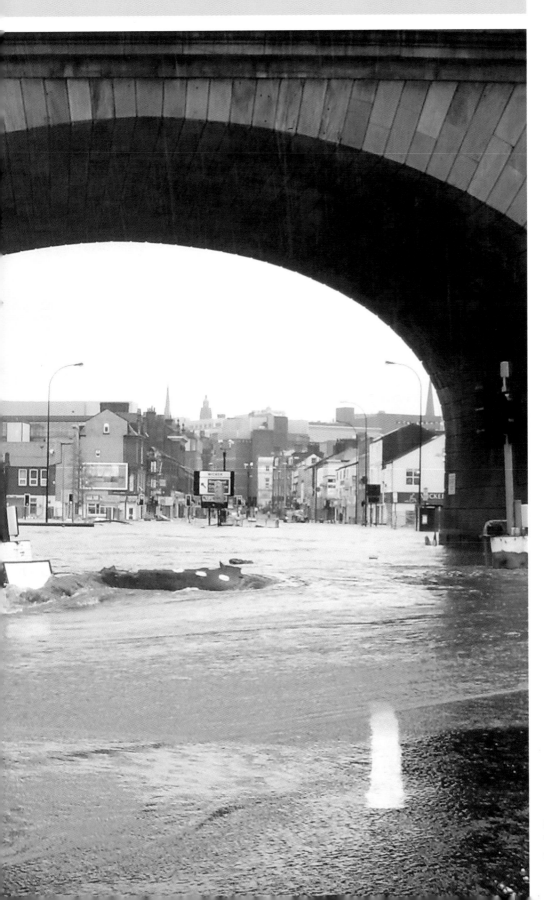

Floods on
The
Wicker.

▲ Battling through flooding, photograph by *Star* reader Granville Charles.

◀

Sheltering under brolleys from the rain.

Floods at Mill Lane houses, Deepcar.

The overflow at Underbank Reservoir, Stocksbridge.

Barnsley Road was closed after heavy rain caused chaos in and around Doncaster.

Many streets in Scawthorpe suffered due to the heavy rain. Cars were brought to a stand still here on Petersgate.

Brodsworth Floods – the Fire and Rescue Service lead residents to safety.

Helicopter rescue.

Floods in Pleasley, north Nottinghamshire.

Francesca Granger carries her neighbour's daughter Amy Jolly, 3, as families are forced to leave their flooded homes in Bentley, near Doncaster. (Pictured supplied by the Press Association)

Flooding in Catcliffe, Rotherham.

Ryan Parry, second from left, minutes before he was swept to his death in Millhouses Park during the floods.

14-year-old Ryan Joe Parry, who died when he fell into the River Sheaf at Millhouses in Sheffield.

CHAOS

DAY 2: By Tuesday, June 26, the full scale of the flood devastation was becoming apparent.

Thousands had been forced to flee their homes, stranded commuters, travellers and the homeless had bedded down beside each other in emergency accommodation all over the city.

Catcliffe and Whiston in Rotherham were devastated. Meadowhall shopping centre was flooded and closed for the week. Sheffield was virtually cut off from the rest of the country as rail and road connections were all but severed.

Worksop and Chesterfield town centres were flooded, no-go areas, thousands of homes were without electricity, many were evacuated as the waters continued to rise, homeowners and tenants blasted councillors for delays in handing out sandbags.

Families with children and the elderly left their homes and belongings and slept in schools, the universities, clubs and community centres.

And still the rain fell.

Not as intensely or as consistently but enough to maintain an air of impending disaster and hamper recovery and rescue work.

But the floods also brought out the best in people.

Tales of heroism and defiance filled the pages of *The Star*.

A pregnant woman was rescued from flood waters in Chesterfield. Ten-month-old Zaynah Khan was saved from her flooded home in Chapeltown. Mountain rescue volunteers took 40 old people to safety from a residential home in Rotherham.

Workers were turned away from flooded factories – if they could get there – and many small companies feared going out of business altogether.

Ulley Reservoir was becoming more of a concern after cracks developed in its dam wall. Fire crews from 17 areas sent in specialist pumping teams to help lower water levels.

In the House of Commons Sheffield MPs raised the question of financial support from the Government to help with the aftermath of the flooding disaster.

Questions were starting to be asked of the city council and rivers authority as to the quality of the city's flood defences.

But the people battled on. They went to work, helped their neighbours, mopped up, baled out and dug in.

They carried on their lives as best they could and prayed for the rain to stop.

UNDER SIEGE

Hundreds still without homes and electricity in floods devastation

The Star FLOOD CRISIS

'The Blitz spirit has prevailed ... people are feeding each other' Reports Pages 2-10

The Star, Wednesday June 27, 2007

▲ Abandoned cars in Brightside Lane, Sheffield.

▶ This one's a write-off! In Brightside Road, one of the worst hit areas of Sheffield.

Debris blocks the River Don outside the Meadowhall Centre.

Under water the groundfloor of the Meadowhall
Centre as you've never seen it before.

Nursery Street, Sheffield, flooded after the River Don rose and burst its banks following several days of torrential rain.

The Wicker
flooded.

Kelham Island
under water.

Floodcopter carrying sandbags to take to beseiged homeowners.

GANGWAY 13

"GRASS GROWS
BY THE INCH
BUT
IS DESTROYED
BY THE FOOT"
PLEASE KEEP OFF
THE GRASS

EMERGENCY EXIT

Hillsborough home of Sheffield Wednesday football club. Steve Kiddy, headgroundsman, looks forlorn as his pitch is lost under three feet of muddy water.

Hillsborough. Get the message?

Another picture from Hillsborough.

Rush Hour in South Yorkshire and the M1's empty due to the crisis at Ulley Reservoir which was threatening to burst its banks – resulting in its colosure through the county.

Water, water everywhere but not a drop to drink... The Plough pictured at Catcliffe, under water.

More floods in Catcliffe.

Battling through. (Picture by *Star* reader Shaun Deaves)

Floods at Mill Lane houses, Deepcar.

Catcliffe floods.

Vacant possession, indoor swimming pool included! Catcliffe.

Catcliffe floods.

Catcliffe floods. Roof of car barely visible under several feet of water.

Fire and Rescue service with their dinghy outside the Bay Horse pub, Bentley.

Truck battles its way through Barrow Road, Wincobank.

People from Rotherham taken from their homes to Herringthorpe Leisure Centre.

Falding Street, Chapeltown, flooded again, with skips full of debris from houses.

First floor almost submerged following flooding at Treeton.

Rotherham residents taken from their homes to Dinnington Comprehensive School.

Feeling the strain: Rotherham residents sit out the flood at Dinnington Comprehensive School.

Star reader Stuart Harrison's photograph of a dog outside Chapeltown Spar Shop on Lound Side.

Ulley Reservoir, where a large scale pumping operation using hose pipes and heavy duty pumps battled to get water levels down as the reservoir's dam threatened to burst.

Ulley Country Park. Emergency services lined up along the road.

Ulley Country Park.

"Hello, you'll never guess where I am." Man caught in floods at Hall Lane, Barrow Hill.

Floods? No problem for these two on bikes on the A60 at Warsop.

Tickhill floods – aptly named Water Lane.

Rain stopped play at Worksop Cricket Club, Central Avenue.

Kilton Hill, Worksop.

Devastation at home of Roger Stocks, Allen Street, Worksop.

Floods in Central Avenue, Worksop.

Worksop Town cricket ground, Central Avenue.

Hardy Street Bus Station, Worksop.

The village of Toll Barr near Doncaster. Residents pack what they need and go.

Help is on the way for
people of Toll Barr.

Leger Way,
Dinnington.

BATTLING THROUGH

DAY 3: As the area muddled through the water, debris and stench a second wave of flood problems began to bite by Wednesday June 27.

The M1 Motorway was closed between junctions 32 and 34 as Ulley Reservoir continued to cause concern.

Firefighters battled on to pump water out of the reservoir and Treeton, Ulley and Whiston were evacuated in case the cracked dam gave way and spilled millions of gallons of water onto the villages below.

By Wednesday night Sheffield was a traffic disaster.

With many outlying roads blocked or only partially passable, getting through Sheffield was almost impossible.

Commuter journeys which normally took half an hour were taking three hours, every road into and out of the city was choked at peak times. For many traffic was the least of their worries.

Some had lost their possessions, cars and even their homes.

In areas like Catcliffe and Whiston people could not go back to their homes and were still living in emergency or temporary accommodation.

Water was still up to first floor levels in the worst hot spots and anger replaced fear as the dominant emotion as people began to ask more searching questions of those responsible for flood defences.

Ex-Prime Minister Tony Blair offered his condolences, MPs David Blunkett, Clive Betts and Angela Smith were joined by City Council Chief Executive Sir Bob Kerslake and Councillor Harry Harpham in a tour of some of the worst-affected areas of the city and pledged to push for fresh investment.

Twice-flooded people in the Darfield area of Barnsley were told they may not be able to move back into their homes until November.

Pictures of Meadowhall under as much as five feet of water appeared and Sheffield Wednesday's new pitch had become a lake of brown water. *Star* readers sent in their own amazing photographs and videos of the trauma of the previous 48 hours as thousands of personal stories from all across the region began to be heard.

Anger over river defences PAGES 2 & 3

☆ The Star FLOOD CRISIS

- **MPs in tour of city devastation** PAGES 4 & 5
- **Threat to dam easing** PAGES 6 & 7
- **Homeless for months** PAGES 8 & 9

Carried to safety: Catcliffe residents were ferried to their homes to pick up belongings and feed pets after river defences failed   Picture: Ross Parry

FEARS RISE OF LOOTING

Extra police on the streets to protect vulnerable homes

By Claire Lewis and Nancy Fielder

POLICE are patrolling flood disaster zones in South Yorkshire to stop looters ransacking abandoned homes.

Officers are on the streets of the worst-hit areas where homes and business have been evacuated, including Catcliffe, Brightside and the Meadowhall area.

People in the hardest-hit areas are outraged anybody would want to steal from homes which the owners are not even allowed into.

Tracey Birch's house in Catcliffe is still underwater and she is furious thieves would choose to capitalise on such a terrible situation.

"This kind of thing makes you feel sick," she said. "This is the most vulnerable time when your homes are most at risk and to go looting in this situation is just the lowest of the low."

Valerie Ripley remembers terrible looting last time Catcliffe suffered serious flooding and said this time round some neighbours have had property stolen from their garden after they put them in the open air to dry out. Other residents claimed their neighbours had been targeted by opportunist gangs of thieves. In Treeton police community support officers stopped some people entering the village yesterday and asked them to identify themselves to ensure looters were not heading for abandoned homes.

Police are on the lookout for anyone hoping to take advantage of houses left in a hurry by residents fleeing the floods.

South Yorkshire Police said there have been no reports of looting but they were aware of concern among residents and have put extra officers on the streets.

Acting Deputy Chief Constable Bob Dyson said anyone seeking to profit from the flooding crisis should be ashamed. "There have been rumours of burglaries and thefts from empty homes but we have not received any reports of this," he said.

"In fact the crime rate is lower than normal because of the impact of the floods and the weather.

"We have extra patrols in areas where evacuations have been carried out by local authorities, meaning we have a high visibility in properties affected by the floods.

"Anyone who chooses to commit

Continues on Page 3

Struggling through the floods at The Wicker.

Star reader Martin Cotton's picture of cyclist outside post office sorting depot at Brightside.

Philippa Jones of Millgate, Bentley, cleans up after the flood. ▲

◄

Susan Baldwin of New Street, Bentley, peers out of her front door which is sandbagged against possible flooding.

Claire Prescott pictured in her Bentley florists 'Mrs Bouquets' which is filled with floodwater.

Pictured at the rear entrance to the shop with her daughter Georgia, aged 10.

Local residents brave the floodwater in Hunt Lane, Bentley.

This pedestrian still observes the Green Cross Code, waiting for the lights to change to red. High Street, Bentley.

Chris Hulme, of 'Stop 'n' Snack', Cooke Street, Bentley, fed and watered flood victims and rescue services during the flood.

BENTLEY FLOOD WATER

This Cloudy vintage was
Bottled in a street near you.

Bottled on Friday 29th June 2007
@ 20.15 from New Street

Bottled by Shawn Wakefield

Assistant Scout Leader, Shawn Wakefield in New Street, the source of his bottled flood water, which is being auctioned off on Ebay, to raise funds for flood victims.

◄

Residents of Ward Avenue clear up after the floods. ▲

Local teenagers mucking around during the floods in Bentley.

Lorraine Milner of 'Lorraine's Barber's', in High Street, Bentley, makes her way to the car park at the rear of High Street, after wading through the floodwater to check out the condition of her business.

Sand bags trying to fill the gaps at an OAPs centre in Ecclesfield, Chapeltown.

Emergency services battling with the elements to rescue people from their homes in Toll Barr near Doncaster.

"I'm on my way but I think I might be a bit late." Wading through the streets of Toll Barr near Doncaster.

Gemma Emmerson, of Manor Estate, Toll Bar, with her one year-old daughter Ruby Lea Copeland-Emmerson, who have been sleeping at Adwick Leisure Centre whilst their home was under flood water.

Firefighters save a dog as
flood waters rise in Toll Bar
near Doncaster.
(Photograph supplied by
the Press Association)

A cyclist rides through the
floodwater outside
Westminster House, Intake,
Doncaster.

A Chinook helicopter carrying sandbags as it flies past a flooded power station on its way to line the river bank near Doncaster. (Photograph supplied by the Press Association)

Two lads paddle their inflatable boat in the floodwater in Sprotbrough Road at its junction with York Road in Doncaster.

Treeton floods.

◄

The long walk home for this commuter on Abbeydale Road South, near the junction with Dore Road.

▼

There's no place like home: Floods in Chapel Walk, Catcliffe.

Boats were used to move people around Catcliffe.

▲

Kerry Neale
wades through
Worksop's
Priorswell Road
floods after
collecting
daughter Isobel
from nursery.

▶

School kids
have a whale
of time.

Flood at Hady Hill, near Chesterfield.

The Wicker debris... Five Weirs Walk sign flattened by the wave of floodwater that poured along the Don Valley.

Caught in the net: Fish in the street on The Wicker after the floodwater subsided.

Staff at Sheffield's Kelham Island start cleaning up after the flood.

Clean up in Winn Gardens, Middlewood, Sheffield.

Clean up begins in Riverside Court, Brightside.

River Don debris blocks the way at Brightside.

Choked: Five Weirs walkway blocked by flood debris.

A Meadowhall food store throwing out bags of wasted food.

Clean up in Winn Gardens, Middlewood.

The clean up continues in Winn Gardens, Middlewood.

▶

Doncaster **NHS**
Primary Care Trust

Health advice during the flooding

The risk of health problems arising from the floods are small, providing you take these sensible precautions:

DON'T come into contact with floodwater where possible.

DO use protective clothing, such as wellingtons and rubber gloves, when cleaning up.

DO wash your hands with soap and clean water before eating food and after cleaning up.

DO clean contaminated areas with soapy water followed by disinfectant.

Drinking water has not been affected and is entirely safe.

Detailed advice is available on the HPA website www.hpa.org.uk.

If you feel unwell ring NHS Direct on 0845 4647or your family doctor for advice. NHS Direct can also give you the contact numbers for local NHS services.

If you are evacuated from your home please make sure that you take your medication with you.

Health advice notice on High Street, Bentley, now cleared of floodwater.

Mayor of Barnsley, Councillor Len Picken, delivers new furniture and white goods to Joanne Forrest-Spain in Lundwood, Barnsley, following the floods.

Scott Oldfield and daughter Lucy at Catcliffe.

▶

The Chinook takes off with a load of sandbags to shore up the banks of the River Don at Almholme.

REACTION AND REFLECTION

DAY 5: By Friday the great and the good were flying in to South Yorkshire to offer moral support and a comforting word to those suffering most in the floods.

Prince Charles came to Catcliffe and showed genuine compassion and empathy with the people still struggling to come to terms with the devastation and their losses.

On a second visit he made a donation from his own pocket to the people of Doncaster suffering the worst of the disaster.

New Prime Minister Gordon Brown also came to Doncaster and was berated by an angry resident who voiced the community's anger at the lack of action to help those who suffered most in the floods.

He spoke for the whole region when he shouted at Gordon Brown: "I'm speaking up for the working man. We've paid our taxes all our lives and now we need something back."

Gordon Brown offered a £14 million rescue package for flood damage victims all over the country.

Tales of heroism were still coming to light including a man known only as Darren who plunged into the floods in a vain attempt to rescue Peter Harding in Sheffield. Darren managed to pull 68-year-old Peter from the churning waters but he was already dead.

Meadowhall was set to re-open a week after it closed following a huge clean-up operation that made most of the mall safe and usable. Some sections of the shopping centre were expected to be closed for months to come.

Doncaster Rovers announced they will use the sell-out pre-season friendly against Manchester United to raise cash for the disaster fund.

The town's mayor Martin Winter, who earlier admitted he felt as though he had let down the people of Doncaster, announces that some may never be able to go back to their homes again, such was the damage wrought by the floodwater.

Others are facing up to the news that they won't be able to return to their houses until next year.

The Environment Agency announced plans for a shake-up of Britain's drainage systems to prepare for the worsening effects of climate change.

Too little, too late for thousands of South Yorkshire, north Nottinghamshire and North East Derbyshire families who know only too well what it means to live with a changing climate.

The Star

Serving South Yorkshire

Saturday, June 30, 2007 **FLOOD SPECIAL EDITION** 38p www.thestar.co.uk

SPORT

BRUNT 'WILL NOT QUIT'

BACK PAGE

THE GREAT FLOOD OF 2007

All the dramatic pictures from this devastating week

16-PAGE SPECIAL FREE INSIDE

Horrified Charles 'to use his influence' for better defences

PRINCE FLOOD GUARD PLEDGE

EXCLUSIVE
By Richard Marsden and Nick Ward

PRINCE Charles has promised to lobby for better flood defences in South Yorkshire - as the county today battened down the hatches for more heavy rain this weekend.

The prince's pledge was made on a visit to Sheffield's Forgemasters steelworks in Brightside, deluged with water when the River Don overflowed its banks on Monday.

The prince also toured sodden Catcliffe, where he told residents swilled out of their homes how he "felt deeply" about the "misery and horror" they suffered.

Met Office forecasters have issued a weather warning to last until 6am

tomorrow, and are predicting further downpours across the country. Although the heaviest rainfall is now expected in the West Midlands and South West, between 15 and 25mm is still due in South Yorkshire.

Authorities across the county are gearing up for the potential of more flooding, because the ground is still saturated while rivers are nearly full.

Touring Forgemasters, Prince

Charles - who described the devastation as "incredible" - said he would "use his influence" to boost defences on the River Don to lessen the risk of future floods.

Sheffield Council leader Jan Wilson, who accompanied Charles on the visit,

said: "He seemed very keen to follow up what he could do to help. He was extremely supportive."

Half a mile from the steelworks, where Meadowhall Road passes

Continues on Page 2

Sympathy: Prince Charles visits the wrecked home of Sally Breeze

Severe disruption in Royal Mail strike

POSTAL deliveries in South Yorkshire have been severely disrupted by the first national Royal Mail strike in over a decade.

Picket lines were mounted outside mail centres and sorting offices from 3am in the dispute, which arose after workers rejected a proposed pay rise of 2.5 per cent. The Communication Workers Union said 95 per cent of its members took part.

■ A SECTION of the M1 was down to one lane today after a two-car crash.

Police closed two lanes northbound and one lane southbound between junctions 34 and 35. Officers said it re-opened around 6.30am and only one person suffered minor injuries during the smash.

The Star, Saturday June 30, 2007

Turf being laid on the Hillsborough pitch after the floods.

Pictured at the T and G Headquarters, Meadowhall, where MP's and council officials met to view the area of the floods. Seen left to right are, Bob Kerslake, Angela Smith, Clive Betts and David Blunkett.

Mina Jamshid Nejad and dog Jack return home to Winn Gardens, Middlewood.

The Prince of Wales visits Forgemasters flood area, Brightside Lane, Sheffield.

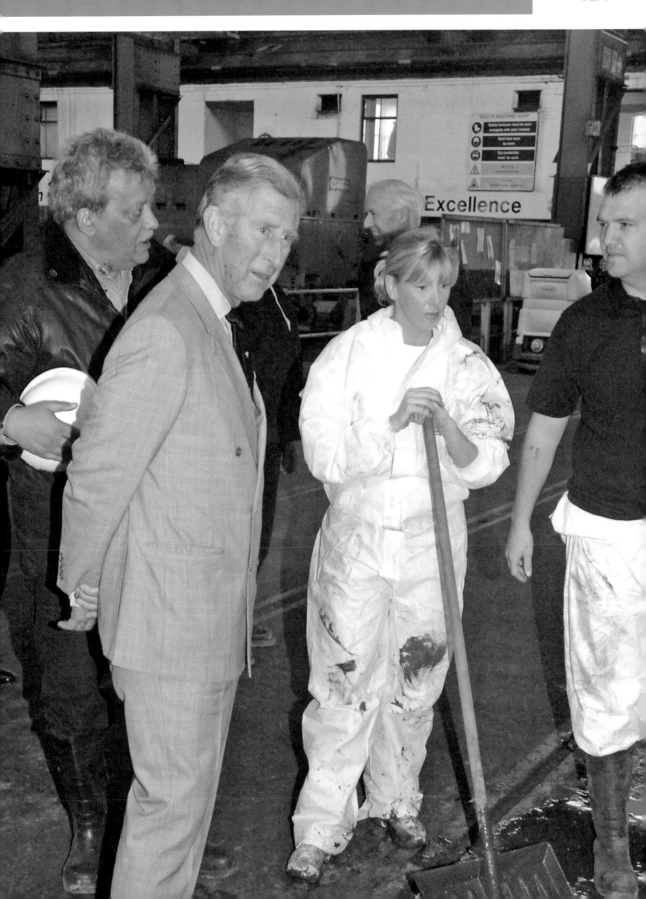

Prince of Wales seen chatting with Forgemasters' Chief Executive Graham Honeyman, left, and staff.

Rob O'Brien from Campsall Working Men's Club delivering aid for flood victims to Adwick Leisure Centre.

Toll Bar resident David Howard is comforted by his wife after being led away by police as he tried to confront Prime Minister Gordon Brown.

Toll Bar resident David Howard pleads for help from Prime Minister Gordon Brown.

Prime Minister Gordon Brown in Toll Bar, near Doncaster, in the aftermath of the floods.

It's question time for Gordon Brown as he meets residents of Toll Bar and Bentley in Doncaster.

Prime Minister Gordon Brown speaks to ▲
the Mayor of Doncaster, Martin Winter,
on a visit to Toll Bar, near Doncaster.

◄

The Prime Minister shares some light-hearted chat with a
resident of Toll bar.

▲ Ryan Parry's funeral. The cortege arrives at Gleadless Methodist Church, White Lane.

▶

Ryan's coffin is carried into the church.

The Reverand Beverley Barclay, Gleadless Methodist Church, White Lane.

Tearful friends and family are gathered to pay their respects to Ryan Parry and left heartfelt messages to a 'loveable lad'.

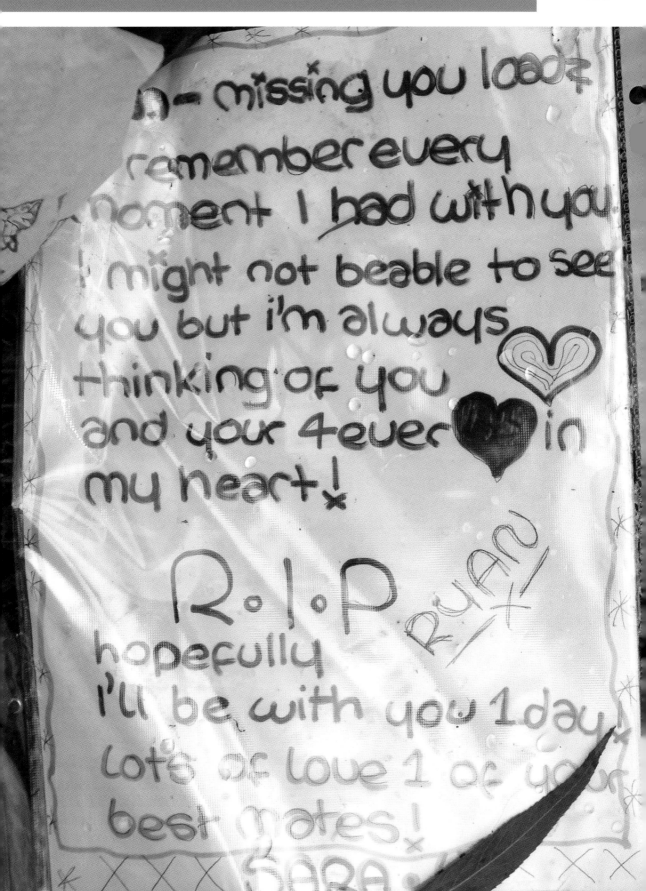

The Reverand Beverley Barclay takes a balloon at Ryan Parry's funeral at Gleadless Methodist Church, White Lane.

Tributes to Ryan Parry in Millhouses Park.

St John the Baptist Church, Church Lane, Clowne. Funeral of Gary Priestley, 51, who died in the floods.

Derbyshire TIMES

www.derbyshiretimes.co.uk

52p   Thursday, June 28, 2007   **CHESTERFIELD/CLAY CROSS**

FLOODS PICTURE SPECIAL
PAGES 2, 3, 4 & 5

WIN! Top cricket prize and tickets to Legoland Live! Page 20

BABY RESCUE FLOOD DRAMA

COMMUNITY spirit prevailed across north Derbyshire this week as hundreds of people battled against rising flood water to save lives and homes – including a hero who floated a six-month-old baby to safety in a tray.

Paul Gilbert (31) was helping his mum at severely flooded Tapton Terrace, Chesterfield, on Monday afternoon, and was checking on her neighbours when he found Anne Squires and her baby daughter Arwen trapped in another property.

by
Jon Cooper

Quick-thinking Paul nestled the baby on a metal tray and pushed her out of the swamped property over four-and-half foot deep, rat-infested water and sewage after the River Rother burst its banks.

Anne said: "It was frightening. The water kept going higher and was above the garden fence and it was too deep to carry Arwen.

"We were scared and thought we might be abandoned, but Paul was wonderful and we will always be thankful for what he did."

Quick-thinking Paul nestled the baby on a metal tray and pushed her out of the swamped property over four-and-half foot deep, rat-infested water and sewage after the River Rother burst its banks.

Her mum and a friend helped to get Persia to safety before Paul stepped into the breach and guided Anne out, with baby Arwen on

"The firefighters told me I shouldn't have been in the water, but I had to help because the people on this road are my friends."

– Rescuer Paul Gilbert

Anne (22) had been at her home on Tapton Terrace when the flooding started but moved to her mum's property on the same road with daughters Arwen and four-year-old Persia. As waters rose, they became trapped.

the tray, over rising floods and uneven ground.

Paul, of Eastside Close, Whittington Moor, said: "The water was getting to shoulder-height so I got the tray, put in cushions and turned it into a raft and pushed the baby across the flood to safety.

"The firefighters, who were brilliant, told me I shouldn't have been in the water and when I think how bad I am at swimming they were right, but I had to help because the people on this road are my friends."

Derbyshire firefighters evacuated about 30 people from the terraced houses, and praised Mr Gilbert for his actions and for guiding crew members to other trapped residents.

The swollen rivers Hipper and Rother burst their banks on Monday and swept though homes in Tapton, Brampton and Spital.

● Turn to pages 2/3/4/5 for more flooding stories and pictures.

jon.cooper@derbyshiretimes.co.uk

● Anne Squires with baby Arwen and hero Paul Gilbert outside the flooded homes at Tapton Terrace. *SP64177*

STORE BLAZE

Firefighters from across north Derbyshire were called out to battle a large blaze at a town-centre supermarket.

The fire broke out at the Somerfield store, in The Pavements Precinct shopping centre, Chesterfield, at 1.30pm, yesterday.

Sean Mahony, station manger based at Chesterfield Fire Station, described the blaze as 'a major incident'.

He added: "Initially there were some reports that people were missing, but now everyone has been accounted for."

All the shops around the Low Pavement area were evacuated as a precaution and the market area was cordoned off.

Firefighters in breathing apparatus were called out to the smoke-logged building from stations in Chesterfield, Staveley, Dronfield and Clay Cross.

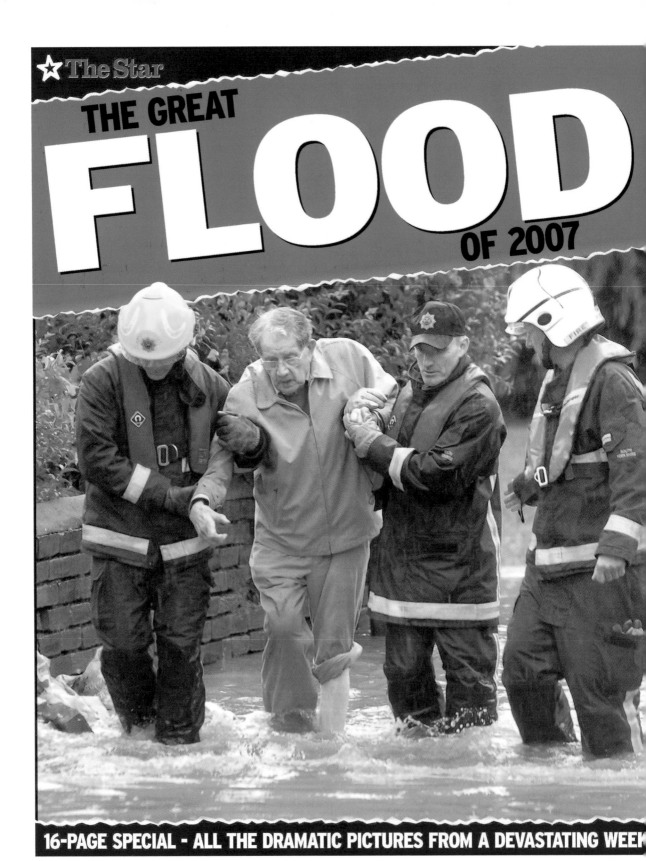

THE GREAT FLOOD OF 2007

★ The Star

16-PAGE SPECIAL - ALL THE DRAMATIC PICTURES FROM A DEVASTATING WEEK

The Star, Saturday June 30, 2007

Guardian

NM **FASTEST GROWING WEEKLY (15,000 - 25,000) IN UK**

Baby of the Year 2007

Get ready for Baby Of The Year p26

Only 2 DAYS To Go!

Bassetlaw gears up for smoking ban p10

Clumber in the Age Of Elegance p22&23

Killed in floods

A CLOWNE father was killed by a lorry as he braved Monday's floods on his bicycle.

Retired police officer Gary Priestley, 51, of Mansfield Road, regularly cycled the route as part of his love of keeping fit –but decided to do so in the floods to avoid damaging his car.

Wife Dawn paid tribute to her 'soul mate and best friend' this week.

Full story on page five

DEVASTATION

Seven-page Guardian insight into floods

South Yorkshire Times

Thursday, June 28, 2007   Serving the community since 1877   www.southyorkshiretimes.co.uk   32p

Flood stories and photographs

See pages 2, 4 and 5

Vandals target castle again

Misery at tea rooms—p7

Meet Dearne's Billy Elliot!

Dancing king - p3

■ 40-PAGE PROPERTY GUIDE   ■ 28-PAGE MOTOR GUIDE   ■ TV PAGE 12   ■ SPORT STARTS PAGE 33

COME HELL AND HIGH WATER

County in crisis after a second week of floods

SOUTH Yorkshire is today beginning its long journey back to normality after the worst floods in living memory.

While Sheffield, which has seen the worst of the bad weather, remains in crisis, the situation elsewhere in the county is beginning to ease.

Many of the major roads which were closed due to the flooding, including Low Road in Conisbrough and Doncaster Road in Denaby Main, have now re-opened.

And residents of Conisbrough and Mexborough who were evacuated from their homes have been allowed back.

But there still remains the risk that the Ulley reservoir near Rotherham could burst, which would have devastating knock-on effects for towns and villages along the River Don.

● For more on the flooding, see pages 2, 4 and 5.

The South Yorkshire Times, Thursday June 28, 2007

Yorkshire's National Newspaper

YORKSHIRE POST

45p FINAL EDITION | www.yorkshirepost.co.uk | WEDNESDAY JUNE 27 2006

OPERATION DAMBUSTERS
THE STORY IN WORDS AND PICTURES OF YORKSHIRE'S WORST FLOODS

Who will pick up the bill?

Swamped: An aerial view of the village of Catcliffe, near Rotherham – under water yesterday after heavy rain caused extensive flooding in the region.   Picture: Owen Humphreys/PA.

Miliband rejects calls for help with flood clean-up costs amid row over defences

Simon McGee Political Editor
and **Tom Smithard**

A FURIOUS row about aid for the flood-devastated areas of Yorkshire erupted last night as thousands of people remained homeless – and a desperate battle continued to prevent a dam smashing millions of tons of water surging through houses and a power station.

Demands for extra financial help for the wrecked communities were brushed aside by Environment Secretary David Miliband, who offered only standard emergency funds to help with the clean-up, which will cost hundreds of millions of pounds.

He was also accused of ignoring experts' warnings about inadequate flood defences.

Mr Miliband claimed the warning system had worked well and there were no reported defence failures.

As the row continued thousands of people in South and East Yorkshire were facing another night in emergency shelters, while those able to return found their homes ruined by water and sewage and were without power.

It came as emergency services continued to battle against the floods brought on by unprecedented rainfall in the region causing rivers to break their

Breach fear: A firefighter monitors hoses draining water behind the Ulley dam near Rotherham.

banks – such as in Catcliffe, near Rotherham, where water was up to the top of garages.

But as the region began to count the cost there were serious question marks over how much help the Government would give hard-pressed councils which had struggled to cope.

Opposition MPs piled further pressure on the Government, claiming the Environment Agency had been forced to make cuts in its flood protection budget last year to compensate for "financial mismanagement" in the Department for Environment, Food and Rural Affairs (Defra).

David Curry, Skipton and Ripon

MP and former Tory Environment Minister, said his constituents felt "anger and frustration" that there had been flood plans in place for many years but each year they were "deferred".

Leeds Council also vowed to put pressure on Defra to resurrect a £100m flood defence scheme for the city that had been shelved for three years.

Hull Council leader Carl Minns said: "The clean-up is going to cost millions of pounds in Hull and the Government has to provide emergency aid. No council will be able to meet the costs needed from its own budget."

Last night many towns

remained under water, major roads were out of action and hardly any trains were running, bringing a second day of chaos for commuters.

About 2,500 homes were evacuated, including 1,400 in Sheffield, and about 66,000 homes were without power. Only 40,000 had been restored by yesterday afternoon.

Insurance claims were up by 800 per cent on the numbers expected for the time of year, with more than 8,500 claims received in 24 hours.

Seventeen specialist fire crews from across the UK were last night battling to stop a 36-acre

Victorian reservoir at Ulley, near Rotherham, bursting its banks and destroying three villages close to Sheffield, part of the M1 and an electricity substation.

The torrential downpour cost the lives of three people from Yorkshire, including Ryan Parry, 14, of Gleadless, Sheffield, who fell into the River Sheaf at Millhouses, and a 68-year-old man who was swept away on Carlisle Street in central Sheffield as he tried to cross the road.

Michael Barnett, 28, died after getting stuck while trying to unblock a drain in Astral Close, Hessle, near Hull.

Elsewhere, police discovered a body in a submerged car near Dewsbury, Worcestershire, where they had spent the day searching for a motorist who had been overwhelmed by floodwaters.

In East Yorkshire people were warned not to leave their homes "unless absolutely necessary", with hundreds evacuated from Hull, Holderness and Grimsby. It was a similar picture in Pickering, North Yorkshire, and in the Aghriggross of Wakefield.

Last night weather forecaster Piers Corbyn said he had warned weeks ago of a downpour between June 24 and 26.

He said further flooding is expected over July 4-6 and July 10-11.

FLOOD CHAOS – PAGES 4, 5, 6, 7 AND 8 ■ **FOCUS P13** ■ **COMMENT P14**

45p ISSN 0963-1496

Bright intervals.
A few showers.
Full forecast: Back Page

0113 243 2701

News 8736
Sport 8473
Business 8969
Features 8950

Yorkshire Post, Wednesday June 27, 2007

EPILOGUE

THE damage and the stench will linger for months, rebuilding will take years, but the memories will never fade.

Just as everyone who has grown up in Sheffield has a notion of the Great Sheffield Flood of March 1864, anyone living and growing up in this city and this region in future will know of the Great Flood of 2007.

Heroism, tragedy, triumph and disaster marked the summer and anyone who lived through it will hope never to see its like again.

The floating cars, stranded workers airlifted from factory roofs, mothers wading through brown waters carrying their children, ruined homes and factories, closed motorways, fish on The Wicker.

There has never been anything quite like it in this area, probably not in this country, on such a scale.

But the chances are we will see many more summers like this one.

Changing world weather patterns suggest that heavy, monsoon-style rain will be a regular visitor to this country and this area.

This Great Flood of 2007 was a warning.

A warning to builders contemplating developments on flood plains, to councils and waterways authorities who must now look to greatly improve our drainage and flood prevention systems, to families and businesses looking for property.

Perhaps no-one could have forseen rains like these, maybe no system could have been expected to cope with storms and volumes of water four times heavier than the region has ever seen before.

Indeed the downpours of this summer have been described by meterologists as a 'once in a 400 year event'.

But it won't be 400 years before we see another one.

Global warming is a fact. Whether it is caused by human activity is less certain but the effects are the same.

We will need Government help to rebuild and repair the damage and we will need Government help to prepare ourselves to better survive future downpours and extreme weather conditions.

In the names of Ryan Parry, Peter Harding and Gary Priestley we have to learn our lesson and learn it now.

Or they won't be the last names on the death toll of our Great Floods.